POETRY IN THE KEY OF LIFE

By John Regan

FOREWORD

This book represents the poems I have written over the previous ten years. The majority, however, have been written in the last two.

I did think about grouping the poems according to the subjects they were describing. However, I decided not to. Whenever I have bought and read poetry books, I have always liked the difference the turning of a page can bring.

I hope some of these poems resonate and, in the reading, you take something from them.

INFORMATION

The profits from this book will be donated to – The Unicorn Centre, Stainton Way, Hemlington, Middlesbrough, TS8 9LX. Many thanks to anyone who purchased it.

John Regan, 2019.

Find me on Facebook and Instagram.

John Regan – Author

Email – johnregan1965@yahoo.co.uk

The passing of the year, from New Year's Eve and back again. Through all the wonderful seasons.

THE PASSING OF THE YEAR

Evanescent of our year's abode meets fast aurora of the coming chime

With fulgent hopes and promises, a mead beyond the passing sound of time

Through Jack frost's kingdom iced in whitely shroud we climb

Impuissant in the face of nature's governance, or earthly realm sublime

Through ire of the coldest force, it travels and meets the certain coming fate

Towards a springtime new, cut fresh from times eternal sovereign state

While creatures great and small eke out existence, and loitering winter to abate

With buds of promises of things to come, we struggle on through frigid wait

Green shoots anew, lift high their heads and blossom showcase's her face

Celerity of life afresh bounds forward in a myriad throng to join the race

While earthly land in all its pulchritude strides forth, towards a temperate place

As summer's warmth and cheeriness will banish fast the chill before without a trace

The Autumn days and night stretch high and offer up abundant dish for our delight

As time runs fast beyond the briefness of the equinox, and
steals the ever-dying light

A race relentless in its cool pursuit, as heat which warmed
the land takes flight

And kingdom of daytime that once held sway is bowed
before the majesty of night

How tenebrous the evenings now become, how stark the
trees above the icy ground

A lambent invitation beckons kith and kin from distant
shores, to gather all around

And storied visitations from our past press forth, and
memories are dusted down

Refulgent faces coruscate with wondrous glee when
Yuletide wears the crown

The way life smooths away those sharp edges of youth.

PEBBLE ON A BEACH

I'm just a pebble on a beach

Surrounded by a thousand more

And far behind beyond my reach

Another world a distant shore

The edges sharp in early days

Were rounded smooth by life's grand march

And burning embers which often blazed

Are tempered, fixed within my hearth

Yet though I miss those bygone highs

That youthful fire which fanned the flames

I've journeyed on with elder eyes

A wisdom too, and steadfast aim

When wax and wane of lifetime push

Has ground me down with true acclaim

The time and tide and season's rush

Will set me free within the grain

And pass through aeons in timeless bay

Where I'll live on forever more

With myriad who passed this way

An echo on some golden shore

Blank Pages echoes the memories left unwritten after a mother dies when her daughter is still young.

BLANK PAGES

A cerulean landscape shone, the presage to my dawn

The blinding glow of maternal gaze, to which I would be drawn

And souls that would forever beat, in symmetry and time

With heartfelt joy and shared belief, our love began its climb

But then as fate walked forward now, and tugged so tightly at my strings

You stepped from light into the dark, as life unfurled its earthly wings

Your illness crept with stealth and guile and stole away those priceless days

And features that had once burned bright, now hide behind a temporal haze

I long to feel that missing touch, I long to view that wonderous smile

I ache for what was never ours, marooned within my lonely isle

Our memories quill laid down in prime, the ink of life was left to dry

Now only pictures fill my void, and only blackness colours my sky

A paltry link to what I lost, a mother's love, endlessly clings

The pages of life eternally blank, a sentence which forever stings

A light-hearted poem with a profound message. Accept people for who they are, and try not to judge.

BILLY'S TROUSERS

Billy had a problem, it was plain for all to see

A cause of much embarrassment, I'm sure you will agree

No matter what he tried to do, be it braces, belt or more

Rope or string, or metal things, there was a single flaw

He worked for years to fathom it, and come to some accord

He cried and cursed and screamed and worse, he even begged the Lord

Despite his protestations, no matter how he swore

The trousers which he donned each day, would end up on the floor

He wrote to dear Deirdre to ask her for advice

She didn't really understand, she said be more precise

He tried in desperation, with nails and bolts and screws

None of this did anything, his pants ended round his shoes

He thought a length of electric flex might finally win the day

But even this was not enough, his jeans still went astray

He dabbled with hypnosis, and positive thinking too

They failed to help in any way, his consternation grew

He madly typed in Google and trawled the internet

His apprehension rocketed, he finished in a sweat

He went to church confession, and told his story true

Unsatisfied with what he heard, he ended in a stew

The problem Billy really had; he was different than anyone

But so are you, and them and me, and everybody under the sun

Some people wear their trousers high, some others have them low

Some people like to keep their's plain, while others put on a show

He finally met his saviour, an ordinary person in fact

Who told him just to be himself, and not put on an act

And Billy finally realised and packed away his hurt

He lives his life the way he wants, now Billy wears a skirt

The folly of putting your faith in people you possibly shouldn't.

AN ALLEGORY? PERHAPS

Such folly of high magnitude

Such arrant disregard for hope

My plangent noise will drown your feud

Your deeds cannot be washed with soap

Your house of whited-sepulchre

Will you my future dulcify

Or draw my eyes away from care

While nocuous voices justify

Pour scorn on people's ignorance

But we can see you wear no clothes

You wait on prole obedience

And fill our heads with hateful prose

Pull drawbridge high prepare the crew

Boil hot the vats of vitriol

And turn our eyes from worldly view

Then fool ourselves imperial

Set sail for lands that don't exist

And cut the rope which tethers us

A troubling jaunt into the mist

With disregard for scorn or fuss

But if in foolish darkling now

Our swift adieu was proved ill-found

And we have followed your sacred cow

Where futures child has surely drowned

Will you and all your shameful flock

Lay low your heads and beg atone

Or smile at fools and gently mock

Then slip beneath your stately stone

The special love that exists between a mother and her daughter. Told from the perspective of the daughter.

A LOVE SUPREME

A soft and gentle drum beat heralded my dawn,

A warm and welcome ocean, to which I would be drawn.

Your voice a pleasing melody, of honey, sweetened words,

That carried me on winds of love and soared like Hummingbirds.

When once I spied your loving gaze, and mine reflected too,

And childish fingers stretched and fell, like springtime morning dew.

You gripped me in a sacred bond, beyond our worldly scope,

I walked along life's path with you, then stood bereft of hope.

When forced to watch you pass on by, and raindrops clouded sight,

My memories a beacon, when daytime succumbed to night.

Our souls once touched, entwined forever,

And love could never fail.

A yardstick that we measure by, in which all others pale,

When time grew short, and bells began their brief and final chime,

A mother's love that sits supreme, a daughters love sublime.

Those days when you find yourself on the wrong side of a hangover, and it takes you most of the day, if not much longer, to feel human again.

HUMAN AGAIN

I haven't found myself today. I searched so hard but couldn't find.

I wandered lost past breakfast time, and through the shadows of my mind.

I drifted back through memories and plotted courses heading south.

I had no map to guide me on, so used my wits and word of mouth.

I'm not the only one to pass this way, the signs are written in the sand.

A shadow of my future self, concealed within a sleight of hand.

A noise that echoes from the walls, but has no light to guide me home.

I stumble on through mists and fog, a cloud descending as I roam.

But then a chink that ever nears, and brightens up a sullen sky.

It spurs me on beyond my noon, my inner sanctum now is nigh.

And when I land in evening time, my black dog lies, cold and slain,

I'm ready to take on the world once more, I'm back to life, and human again.

Despite the atrocities that terrorists commit around the world, we can't ever let them divide us.

MANKIND UNITE

The death dispensed from bloody gun

Will not detract from goods resolve

Nor dull the gleam of loves great light

Or hopes eternal strength resolve

For we with sinew stretched will fight

Our freedom we will not accede

Though some would seek to test our will

The cowardly kin and hateful creed

We stand stalwart on moral heights

And scream that it was ever thus

We've more that will mankind unite

Than separates the mass of us

If only we could go back in time and say the things we should have said, to people we love.

THE THINGS WE SHOULD HAVE SAID

If we could seize the time long past, and with new words, we wouldn't waste

Our time amongst the day's new cast, or let them fall with reckless haste

We'd surely speak the things once missed, to those that were the most and plea,

So they could see for we'd persist, how very much their love was key

But time will not hand back its gold, restrained within a temporal cell,

And we could never hope to hold or view the land in which they dwell

Our present thoughts are all we own, which gather long within our head

As we look down at seeds unsown and view the words, we should have said.

That special time of the year, when families and friends gather together and recall the memories from Christmas past. And maybe a chance to look forward to more.

YULETIDE JOY

Oh yuletide joy we meet once more

From journeys past, you sing your song

Through timeless seas, my memories pour

And thoughts of those which had belong

And ghosts rub shoulders with corporeal kind

Their faces shine from gilded frames

A love which will forever bind

Despite the dimming of the flame

Of vanished hands and voices too

That wrapped my gifts in wondrous joy

And forged remembrances anew

Where love and happiness employ

But time moves on with reckless glee

No note for tears or solemn glance

And disregard for heartfelt plea

No reins to curb sustained advance

And though we hope there's more to come

Those faces which we haven't met

Of love embrace which will become

The Christmas time of future yet

Though life relentless marches on

The phantoms of our past we stem

We cast our thoughts towards the gone

And bless the time we had with them

A palimpsest is something reused or altered, but still bearing visible traces of its earlier form. I think our memories are like this.

PALIMPSEST

My life in all its glorious quest

With words etched deeply in my past

And as I head towards my rest

That ever nears and quickens fast

The ink which once shone brightly new

Is covered, masked and vaguely set

And layered over as I grew

Its meaning almost lost, but yet

There still retains a vague outline

And though with years is gossamer thinned

I smell the grapes upon the vine

And feel caress of gentle wind

How many more will I put down?

How many years will I be blessed?

'Till pen and quill and once renown

Are lost beneath my Palimpsest

Memories of a wonderful Mother.

A POEM FOR MAM

I sit today and think of you, with time no salve to soothe my pain,

Of bygone days and memories, of bright sunshine and autumn rain.

Of fevered brow and childhood tears, and calming words you whispered too,

And love you showered over me, which never faltered as I grew.

The man I am, the boy I was, have never once forgotten this,

And even though I've journeyed on, I'd never fail or be remiss.

To thank the stars that shone above, and count the blessings one by one,

I cannot measure my depth of loss, or put a value, now you're gone

It is uplifting to think that grandchildren have a small part of their grandparents' make-up within them. Even after we are gone, our genes will be passed on to our descendants in an incredible genetic relay race. Just as we contain remnants of our antecedents, those that come after will carry with them the merest trace of us.

BLOODLINE TREE

The fragileness of life laid bare

Within a time of once before

And dreams and hopes of new-born care

Are pushed through space of loving core

Arrival of a hint of me

Which waited long in breathless awe

Cast stones from past in love decree

And drives the coldest heart to thaw

A tiny branch from bloodline tree

Which carries souls from aeons past

That heard and reached in heartfelt plea

Then showered me in wondrous blast

When time has wiped away my place

And fragments which I carried through

You'll still retain the merest trace

Which flows within the veins of you.

From my book – The Space Between Our Tears – describing the feeling of guilt.

GUILT

Constrict my throat and ache my heart, pull senses back through time's deep sea.

And drown me in waters of long-suppressed, in a bottomless ocean of self-pity.

Nothing can resist its strength, or free me from its iron-clad grip.

The dagger-like stab of memories past, unwelcome fall, defences strip.

Laid bare before this mighty force, a locus where raw power resides.

I give up hope, embrace despair, as dreams are washed away on tides.

Nothing good is left for me, my reason stares, fragile and brittle.

I fall supine and beg forgiveness, subsumed by guilt, I die a little.

There is just no telling what life has in store for us. Waiting around the corner, could be something terrible, or maybe something truly wonderful.

PRICELESS GOLD

Have you enjoyed your life thus far?

Has sunshine filled the bluest sky?

And sparkled through to dazzling star

Which shone so bright on heavenly high

And have you felt a lover's kiss

And joined in hands of your soul-mate

Which beckoned on in precious bliss

As time slipped by in endless fate

Have childish hands enraptured you

Their eyes that gaze in innocent awe

And watched in wonder as they grew

From childlike love to adult shore

Have parents from your lingering past

Aged on but always clung to you

With love that would forever last

And never wavered from the true

And have you felt the sting of loss

That painful stab of lost someone

A heavy and a ponderous cross

The teardrops shed with setting sun

Your life in vibrant tapestry

With moods and colours of yet untold

May fashion more of agony

Or coat your life in priceless gold

The doubts we sometimes harbour.

TERRA INCOGNITA

The clouds that once had lifted have drifted back today.

With leaden feet, they creep across, my warm and sunny bay.

My destination, once in view, now masked within a haze.

The clarity of thoughts once held, orphaned within its maze.

Tossed headlong into seas of doubt, forsaking my isle of lone.

Every step and footfall, further away, from my now retreating throne.

And dormant feelings, long suppressed, have now begun to stir.

Their potency a troubling tumult, of almost forgotten care.

I don't know where I'm heading, or what waits along the road.

My thoughts a rising tide of fear, its weight a ponderous load.

And blue touch paper inevitable, join forces with the flame.

A mirror pushed before me, and no one else to blame.

Will time with all its moods and colours be gentle with my hand?

Or will I forever rue the day, I ventured from this land?

Those moments in life where unhappiness pays you a visit, and you find it hard to pull yourself out of it.

NO LONGER BLUE

Pour yourself a glass of self-pity, and pull up a chair

Raise a tumbler up high, and let's toast our despair

I'm on my way to oblivion, you can come if you dare

Leave your hopes and your dreams, because we haven't a prayer

I know what you're thinking, it's clear as a bell

If we head down this road, we're heading for hell

If I end up in Hades, I'll happily dwell

It has to be better than being walled in this cell

But look to the sky, what's this I see?

A sparkle of sunshine, heading for me

A slither of land in this torturous sea

A push to the south and I'm hopefully free

Maybe my dark day is finally through

The obituary you're writing might need a review

The rain that was falling is fading from view

I'm happy again, and no longer blue

My mother suffered from dementia and barely recognised her own children before she died. Memories are precious things. One day you may wake up and find someone close to you has been robbed of theirs.

WHERE HAVE ALL THE MEMORIES GONE?

Where have all the memories gone,

Did you put them down, perhaps?

Or did you hide them safe and sound,

Behind a wall or underground,

Did the rental on them lapse?

Did a thief sneak in as darkness fell?

And spirit them away,

Were they exchanged for coins of gold?

Or did you trust someone to hold?

Those priceless gifts from yesterday.

If I could get them back for you,

I'd search the sea, the sky, the lands,

I'd pay a ransom fit for kings,

Hand over all my precious things,

To hold them in my hands.

I only have one wish from you,

One wish before you go,

For you to recognise my face.

A chance to feel the last embrace,

As I walk through the door.

Some journeys in life are worth the shoe leather.

CROSSING MY RUBICON

With eager strides, I step off, across the barren land,

With memories safely vanquished, and hope within my hands.

The distant light that beckons me forever draws me on,

With quickening steps, I ever near and I cross my Rubicon.

The point of no return I dreaded, no longer holds me back,

Yearning for my future self, I push on through the black.

As Moonlight throws its silvery shroud, across the golden sands,

A far-off glow that stretches out, her soft and welcome hand.

I travel on, and meet warm zephyrs, that dance across my skin,

Her brilliance a nearing presence, that slowly sucks me in.

A lush and verdant oasis, out of place among the gloom,

That pushes back retreating thoughts, laying waste to any doom.

And as I push a hand to touch her bright and shining face,

She meets my stare and captures me within her loving grace.

We dance the dance across the age that only lovers do,

Conjoined in timeless symmetry, subsumed in golden hue.

Embraced within her pools of hazel, which forever hold me fast,

My long and arduous journey over, and truly home at last.

We should rejoice at every sunrise. There is a finite number that we can enjoy. One day, the sun will rise in the sky, and we will not be here to witness it.

GOLDEN RISE ASCENT

First light of golden rise ascent

Which heralds loud the day cut fresh from time anew

And Helios in his flaming chariot rides hell-bent

From eastern home to western coup

While Phoebus warms the coldest heart afresh

The daylight splashed across my heart set fair

And nature bound in life enmesh

Illuminated great, with lambent light and heavenly glare

And aeons past, before my eyes could see

Will also pass when time has cast my form in earthly dust

While others who would view the morn with glee

Are swept in time's great spend entrust

When people who remember me have long since gone

My human-kin has fled when race was run

And other people in yet unwritten solar song

Will fast rejoice in multitude and rising sun

The universe is a strange place. Everything within it is made up of atoms. Yet these atoms consist of mostly space. If you removed this space and squashed together what was left, the whole of the earth's population, all seven billion plus, would fit into something the size of a sugar cube.

LIFE IN A SUGAR CUBE

If all the space that lives within

Was taken out and pushed aside

And what was left and there within

With only mass and none beside

And squashed together in solid form

Then earth's great number and multitude

When stripped of this in fast conform

Would fit within a sugar cube

A poem about those floral tributes we far too often see beside roadsides. Marking the site of a loved one who never made it back home to their family. Through the seasons they lie there, reminding us of just how tenuous life is.

It represents a change in my poetic style, away from my usual rhyming couplets.

BEREFT OF HOPE

It lies forlorn, bereft of hope,

A testament to broken hearts,

Silently sleeping on grassy slope.

Dew brushed and wind-blown.

Fulfilment of the greatest fears,

A bouquet of sadness,

Wrapped In a tissue of tears.

Rain sodden and sun-bleached.

What once was, but is no more,

Alone beneath the giant oak,

Cut down in bloom and heartsore.

Frost dusted and leaf-strewn.

As days and weeks and months pass by,

A sideways glance from passing pilgrims,

And raindrops on cheeks begin to dry.

Snow-covered and frozen stiff.

In another place on another day,

At foot of wall or wooden post,

Someone who happened to pass this way,

Personified in floral repose.

As we get older, will we be able to hang onto those beautiful and precious memories from our past? Or will we have lost them?

WHEN TIME AND AGE HAVE CLIPPED MY WINGS

Should I live on to golden years

When time and age have clipped my wings

And curtain call forever nears

Will I still think of childish things?

The memories which once burned bright

Will they have dimmed or lost their flame

Will legacy have taken flight

Those priceless gifts, not mine to claim

I hope that I have clung to you

I hope your face still draws a smile

And recollections gleam like new

To glow and glimmer and stay a while

If I have lost this wonderous geld

I swear to save some piece that's true

Inside my heart steadfastly held

A shadow and the ghost of you

When out and about doing my day job, I ventured into a cemetery nearby. I was inspired to write this poem after noticing a new headstone recently erected, on the grave of a little boy who had died over fifty years ago.

WHEN DO WE STOP SAYING GOODBYE?

A stone that marks a point in time

When flesh and blood were there to see

And though the bells no longer chime

You carry on with thoughts of me

Though even in my tender years

I forged a mark within your heart

No time can dry the passing tears

Or end the pain we spent apart

Now over fifty years have passed

And life has lined your face with age

Your memory of me is still held fast

In mortal life 'till final page

A stinging ache that never ends

As love for me forever ties

A broken heart which never mends

And lasts until your own goodbyes

A poem I wrote in Remembrance of the many who gave up their tomorrows so we could have our today's.

LET US NOT FORGET

Only now when wisdom wipes away the veil of ignorance, and lucidness and clarity join forces in a clarion call.

Do those who made the ultimate of sacrifices still, with glistened eyes belittle not, achievements of their fall?

And we that hoist ourselves above the bodies of the many, and live our lives on crimson carpets of the sacred dead.

Can we if called to arms to fight a noble battle, boldly walk along the path of courage, where hopes and dreams were quickly shed.

A mournful flower blooms within the heart of goodness, illuminating footsteps of those that passed this way.

And never knew the joys of growing old amongst their brethren, or lived to see the setting sun at close of play.

I shut my eyes and lift my head up high upon eleventh hour in remembrance, and bless the gift that you have given me.

A land of green and pleasant country forged by heroes, where children of a golden age walk free

In the Pantheon of love, a Mother's sits on top. Looking down on all the other types of love that foolishly believe they have any hope of supplanting her.

A MOTHER'S LOVE

Oh love of yours which stands supreme

And wraps my world maternally

With lustre of the sharpest gleam

At once set sail in Argosy

And though some other, may dream supplant

Or force you from a realm so bright

Their chance is ever rendered scant

Their hope of such so thin and slight

With foolish eyes and envy high

They hope in vain to cut the cord

Which stretches long in birthday tie

That soft refrain of motherly ward

She will outlast these stubborn foes

And they must just accept defeat

For in their hearts a price is owed

The cost of which is life so sweet.

The origin of this poem has been kicking around in my head since I witnessed an ex-serviceman sleeping rough outside the train station in Edinburgh.

As a country, we should do more.

UNSUNG

I once rode high in golden day, on magic youth and summertime.

And with my comrades I would stray, past morning call to evening chime

The ripest fruit of clarion call, with khaki friends of brotherhood.

And how with oath we all stood tall, with fervent heart of oaken-wood

The cockcrow of my endless fall was forged on fields in adulthood.

In foreign lands of fireball, which cracked the ground on which I stood

When stripped of brethren I called kin, my purpose lost on civvy street.

And life in headlong, great tailspin, grew demons dark of fast accrete

My emptiness finds comfort now, beneath a blanket on the street.

The shadows are my lonely bough, as memories and ghosts compete

The passing people look away, from downcast man with vacant eyes.

As I eke out another day, beneath an ever-darkening sky

This broken soldier who risked his life must battle on in mighty war

'Neath gathering clouds of untold strife, and come to terms with what he saw

My world's inside a bottle now, and opiates can't dull the pain

I stumble on with life somehow and carry on through endless rain

If you had seen my youthful days, you would not view me as you do

I was a son to those that loved, I've been a brother and father too

My face once filled a picture frame, my smile a joy of boyish year

I never saw the ending nigh or heard the toll of bell draw near

My innocence was just a coat, I shed along with lifetime hope

Left bare upon some foreign field, laid down on ground and stygian slope

Now innocence has slipped from me, and age has masked when I was young

I'm now a shell in all but name, unloved, uncared for, unsung

The terrible way we continue to treat our planet and the creatures within it. What will the following generations, our children and great-grandchildren, make of it? Will they be appalled that we sat back and did nothing?

HOW SAD THAT IT HAS COME TO PASS

How sad that this has come to pass

And some should hang their heads in shame

The ordered few and righteous mass

And no one else with which to blame

And Gaia in her saintly seat will grieve

For how we've spoiled our Eden sweet

Across the lands laid waste below our weave

And crushed all hope beneath our callous feet

The ground when once replete in verdant grace

Now stripped of gifts set down in timeless past

As arrant greed and ruthless face

Watch on impervious and seal humanities last

The river clear and crystal spring

And ocean blue a midden for mankind's great heap

Are wastelands now forged deep with suffering

While apathetic politicians sleep

Great lungs that held the breath of life
Are felled with ever-quickening glee
And countless fauna in its multitude at onetime rife
Lay sacrificed on bloody altar of alacrity

The empty-promise demagogues stand by
Indifferent to nature's deafening plea
With global-warming ticking time-bomb nigh
Good sense and wisdom flee

Will history make a mockery of men like these?
And point a wraith-like finger at their lunacy
While mother nature supplicates upon her knees
In readiness for earth's eternal eulogy

Our sons and daughters are left to pay the price
And fast lament that we watched on obligingly
As governments sat back and viewed the sacrifice
Yet never once gave thought to mutiny

It's not necessarily the value of an ancient, unearthed object which captivates the finder. It's the fact that something held in our hands was owned by a person who lived a long time ago. Value, like beauty, is in the eye of the beholder.

BENEATH COLD CLAY

Beneath cold clay, you slept alone

Your beauty hidden from mortal gaze

No trace of kin or whitened bones

A memory teased from bygone days

A thousand years of long goodbye

When someone held you in their heart

In darkened night or bluest sky

The temporal kiss of age depart

Although your charm will not be swayed

Unearthed by hand of present sent

Your worth and merit are now displayed

With awe and love and times augment

And yet it's not the precious need

That captivates those modern eyes

For something else will far exceed

The hand that held when new, which ties

I happened on a stone at the threshold of a door. The middle worn down after years of people walking over it. There are other clues to people long gone if you care to look. A bannister, a handle, an arm of a chair, worn smooth by decades of human intimacy. When we go, there will be objects out there that bear the merest trace of us.

A STONE WORN SMOOTH

A stone worn smooth by nameless feet

How many souls have passed this way?

How many lives now obsolete?

Their whitened bones beneath cold clay

The echoes from another time

Are silent now and laid to rest

And we will wait for dolorous chime

When our lives' care is age divest

A river's birth, from up high amongst the clouds in the form of raindrops, to its final destination, the sea. Gathering pace and strength as it makes its way downwards with ferocity, pushing its way past anything in its path.

HEAVENLY HIGH

My birth was up on heavenly high

Where clouds are born and eagles soar

And with my kin, I drop from sky

In hilltop shower or earthly pour

My brethren many, we coalesce

From gentle brook and flowing stream

And downward through a valley, press

Conjoined by more we gather steam

We scour through rock and slice through soil

And push down valleys verdant green

In timeless roll, in endless toil

Past natures panoramic scene

And as we gather in size and speed

We roil and roll into a swell

Which drops from height as land accedes

That none can halt or hope to quell

And then we nudge past sleepy town

Move giant objects in our path

The land once parched is surely drowned

Then washed away before our wrath

And then with glee, I see the goal

It rises up to gather me

In watery arms, it makes me whole

My resting place the emerald sea

My dad, who suffers from dementia, is in care now. However, every now and then I see a glimpse of the man he was, and I'm reminded of how important he has been in my life.

THE GHOSTS OF PAST

Please tell me how it came to this, the ghosts of past were cast adrift

A lifetime garnered in your smile, a reasoning so bright and swift

My guiding light which now burns dim, when once you held me in your thrall

A spark, a voice, no longer brim, my heart let out a plaintive wrawl

I glimpsed the shadow in your eye, those priceless gifts that life bestows

And watched the dying of the light, and watched the fading of the rose

Insidiously it stole from you, your treasure trove, a lifetimes glee

And left a shadow of a man, no heed to hope or heartfelt plea

No laughter now you've lost that too, so artful was the memory thief

Your fall from grace a rapid one, winged chariots of time so brief

And yet I have to catch my breath, take succour from the time we had

Take comfort from a lifetime lived, and never forget our life, my dad

Included in my book – The Space Between Our Tears – And written after I attended the funeral of a childhood friend on a cold January morning.

THE FINAL JOURNEY

A pall drifts steadily across a sullen winter sky as sunshine bows and takes it's leave.

And Gold and yellow teardrops tumble dolefully, from the stark and naked trees.

Divested and denuded branches, look on and bend their heads in reverence.

While shuffling, mournful pilgrims follow suit in sombre melancholy deference

A sadness falls across a waiting throng, infecting sorrow strips happiness from all around.

As eyes turn left and meet the black and stately ship, which glides towards its final resting ground.

Enormity of loss in splendid oak, through solemn glass, bedecked in floral solitude.

Draws painfully to passage end, a citadel where many mass, a fortress of the blackest mood.

And memories lofted high, on mighty shoulders of the few, march forward on,

Sheep-like kin and friends before, are sucked through door towards the gone.

As death walks tall amongst the living, and follows us all, from birth to wake

A realisation dawns across assembled crowd, a journey that we all must make.

You can't have the rainbow without having the rain. That's what people say. They appear from nowhere and disappear just as quickly. One could even believe that they were never there in the first place. Maybe we just imagined it? Possibly a metaphor for our lives? Their appearance a reminder that behind every shower, there is something better waiting for us.

RAINBOW

As raindrops cease their heavenly fall

And sunshine owns the day

I see you in kaleidoscope hues

That bends in breathless bay

Caressing colours loud and bright

An arc that kisses cloud and sky

That has no depth and has no height

And softly draws a silent sigh

She gently bows her head to us

With playful joy, she lifts a smile

Before with haste and wink of eye

Her Joseph coat and lost beguile

Are gone once more in timeless glee

A ghost of what was never here

Is all that's left for me.

If you're going to fall in love, where better than Whitby?

IN THE SHADOW OF THE ABBEY

Close to the shadow of the abbey, within a saintly hue

Amid the echo of the ancients, a seed was planted and grew

With every break of sunshine, a thought is born anew

How fortunate I was that day, and how deeply I love you

Whitby Bookshop, situated on Church Street, is a joy to visit and browse around. With its snake-like staircase which winds upward, the shop is steeped in the history of this wonderful fishing town.

POSTERITIES PAGE

I know of a bookshop that sits by the sea

Beneath high steps on saintly street

In sight of cliff and ancient quay

Where human form meet ghostly feet

And if you chance to venture toes

That lead through doors toward written word

In search of new or classic prose

And wondrous stories yet unheard

You'll find the King of horror there

Lovecraftian tales that scream and moan

A Barker or Stoker if you dare

And many more to chill to the bone

There are penmen and authors we all know by name

A thrillers Child is within your reach

Or Rankin and Grisham, Rendall and James

And others too, which we could beseech

There are Hardy and Bronte, and Shakespeare too

If love is the quest that you long to attain

Or topics and themes which shine brightly anew

A puzzle, enigma or maybe arcane

And look to the stairs that gather your gaze

They twist, and they turn to the floor that they bond

The sinuous snake-like supported on stays

A gateway to secrets and treasures beyond

They creak, and they groan as you make your ascent

And fingers touch wood from a different age

The shadows of past which were finally spent

And marked out in ink on posterities page

A memory of someone no longer with us – either gone for good or a short time – will sometimes arrive unannounced. Transporting us back to a memory of them, only to disappear just as quickly as life's cares, attract our attention, and the memory of them slips away again.

FORGOTTEN'S WELL

I saw your face again today

It ambled in from far off lands

And tugged at strings within my heart

And touched my soul with distant hands

Transported on a temporal wind

That carried me to lifetime past

Conjoined with you on memory isle

With onetime joy of once held fast

But fleeting light must dim and fade

Quotidian time will break the spell

As thoughts of you slip from my grasp

And tumble down forgotten's well

We are all made from stardust. The elements that made us were formed in the furnaces of long-dead stars, millions or billions of years ago. For the briefest of moments, we live, until we return from where we came. The atoms from our bodies, re-used in a giant cosmic recycling plant.

STARDUST

Beneath the sky azure blue, atop the grass of verdant green.

Within the glow of golden hue, beside the water crystal clean.

Above the clouds of grey and white, within the sight, of far-off stars.

Among the many distant lights, beyond the bright red glow of Mars.

In hear-shot of the faintest sounds, the far side of all we understand.

Remote of all we comprehend, inside of only dreamt of lands.

You'll find a piece of me right there, amid my home of long before.

The stardust of the universe, where I'll again reside once more.

A poem dedicated to my favourite tipple.

ODE TO RUM

Rum, Rum I love you so

You are the bestest drink I know

Whether neat or over ice

Or mixed with Coke you're just as nice

If I could fill a pool with you

I'd strip clothes off and dive right in

Swim about from end to end

Shout and laugh and make a din

And when they finally fished me out

And coroner with bated breath

Would state quite unequivocally

I'm not sure if he drowned, or drank himself to death!

Bad memories are strange things. They lay dormant, gathering dust in the far corner of the mind until a sound, a smell, or a taste beckons them forward. Then they arrive, unannounced and unwanted like an uninvited guest. Transporting you to a time and place you don't wish to be. You can't fight them, though. There's no silver bullet to bring them down, or an impregnable cloak to throw around us. The emotional tsunami has to be ridden out until it abates, and returns to where it came from.

LOST

Where are you hiding today?

In the shadows at the back of my mind

Gathering dust before seeking me out

Turning time and beginning to wind

How can you pull on my strings so tightly?

Or cause raindrops to fall from my sky

Push daylight away and replace it with night

When I've no shield to protect me, or weapons to fight

I can't remember your face

Only the name that I gave you that day

There's a piece of me, I left in that room

My emotional jigsaw, still missing today.

In the battle of the Somme, almost twenty thousand soldiers lost their lives on the first day. As well as commemorating the fallen, we should also remember the stupidity and futility of war. This is my take on that.

PLAINTIVE PLEA

A crimson river flows through time,

Enlists with others to form a sea,

Corrupting all it washes over,

No haven safe nor steadfast lea

Which stretches long, a century length,

No heed to sobs or plaintive plea,

And ghostly faces which once held breath

Are copper-alloyed for all to see,

Or crumpled creased in sepia past,

And forged in words of you and thee

Dug deep within a martyred rest,

As death demands his rightful fee

My girlfriend and I composed this poem while enjoying a nice pint, watching the sun go down over our favourite place to visit.

SUNSET OVER WHITBY

Sunset dies over Whitby bay

A fireball drowning in the sea

As time and sand run out the day

Night throws her cloak across the quay

The ghosts of past slip by unseen

As lighthouse blinks a knowing eye

And black-clad figure of deathly sheen

Steps forth in dark, unearthly cry

46890295R00033

Printed in Poland
by Amazon Fulfillment
Poland Sp. z o.o., Wrocław